D0206797

# CHRISTIAN WOMEN
## IN A
## TROUBLED WORLD

The 1985 Madeleva Lecture celebrates the opening of the Center For Spirituality of Saint Mary's College, Notre Dame, Indiana, and honors the memory of the woman who inaugurated the college's pioneering program in theology, Sister Madeleva, C.S.C.

# CHRISTIAN WOMEN IN A TROUBLED WORLD

## MONIKA K. HELLWIG

1985 Madeleva Lecture
in Spirituality

PAULIST PRESS
New York/Mahwah

Library of Congress
Catalog Card Number: 84-62886

ISBN: 0-8091-2713-X

Published by Paulist Press
997 Macarthur Blvd.
Mahwah, N.J. 07430

Printed and bound in the United States of America

# CHRISTIAN WOMEN IN A TROUBLED WORLD

The series here initiated is dedicated to a great woman, Sister Madeleva of the Congregation of the Holy Cross, and it is the intent of all that is done in her name that other Christian women should come to know and to realize their own potential for greatness. Sister Madeleva was one to appreciate and to practice the sensitivity of poetry, the wisdom of philosophy and theology, and the eminently practical good sense of offering women the best possible education. She was a person who did and a person who inspired, and it is well that neither her deeds nor her inspiration should be lost to future genera-

1

tions. We are heirs to a great legacy and we hold it in trust as capital to be invested productively for the world of our own generation and that of our children's and their children's generations.

## Voices from the Past

Of course, Sister Madeleva was not the first to care greatly about the education of women to take their full responsibility in the world. Even in pagan classical times Plato favored it,[1] and so it seems did the parents of Theano, Diotima, Sappho and Erinna.[2] In Christian times we have the New Testament testimony about deaconesses, prophetesses and women apostles who were founders of churches.[3] We know that the Church Fathers, Origen and Jerome, thought it important to open Christian scholarship to women in the interests of a truly Christian spirituality, and that noted Christian scholars, such as Abelard and Thomas More, committed themselves earnestly to sharing the whole cultural heritage with young girls.

Similarly, when we look through the centuries of Christian history, we find in spite of unfavorable circumstances a surprising number of Christian women whose learning, competence and spirituality made creative and significant contributions to the history of their societies and the history of the redemption of the world. Some well-known ones spring immediately to mind. There are, of course, the great queens, such as Clotilde of the Franks, Margaret of Scotland, Elizabeth of Hungary, and Elizabeth of Portugal. There are the great foundresses and abbesses: Brigid of Ireland, Hilda of

Whitby, Hildegard of Bingen, Gertrud von Hackeborn and Gertrud the Great of Helfta, Teresa of Avila, and, nearer our own times, women such as Elizabeth Seton, Francesca Cabrini, and Janet Erskine Stuart. But there are also the even more extraordinary women who broke through all the stereotypes and did truly unique and creatively redemptive things, each in her own situation and setting—Egeria the Pilgrim, Perpetua the scholarly martyr, Hadewijch of Brabant, Bridget of Sweden, Catherine of Siena, Julian of Norwich, Margery Kempe, Catherine of Genoa and many more. There have also been the extraordinary reformers, envisaging transformation of social structures, or sometimes bringing them about almost by accident—people such as Elizabeth Fry, Octavia Hill, Frances Cobbe, Josephine Butler, Dorothy Day, Clara Lubich, Catherine de Hueck and Mother Teresa of Calcutta.[4]

Yet it must be admitted that in spite of all these splendid women, we have only fragments of a "usable past" when we look to the tradition for guidance and inspiration in shaping a spirituality for Christian women in the troubled world of our times. We are not lacking in prayer traditions, though there is still some tendency for these to be either monastic in origin and diluted for lay people, or lay in origin but tending to devotional expressions not centered upon the great mysteries of salvation and tending rather to the peripheral. We are not lacking in traditional teachings concerning the Christian virtues, but these tend to point women toward submission in Church, society and family, and therefore tend to become counsels of passivity. They tend to understate and to obscure the potential and the vocation of Christian women in the troubled world of our actual human history.

## WHAT HISTORY REVEALS

This problem is in one sense a general one. The earliest Christians lived in a world that did not know democracy and had not taken critical note of its economic and social systems. In that world they were not purely passive, but it often seems to us retrospectively that they were so. Actually, as more critical appraisal shows us, the early Christians, both men and women, were quite creatively revolutionary in their approach to human society as they knew it and saw it around them. We learn from the Acts of the Apostles and from the letters of Paul that these Christians structured their own communities in totally new ways. They rejected all formalities, distinctions and separations which might interfere with total community. As they understand the spirituality of Christians, property and resources are held in trust for those in need, so there can be no divisions in their society based on the distinction of rich and poor. The truth is more important than winning an argument; the society of the followers of Jesus must share its faith, hope and concerns so that the truth can be shared fully in charity. The only kind of leadership that is in accord with the good news of Jesus Christ is that of ministry, of service, not of domination, and therefore there is no need of titles of respect to establish psychological distance. Moreover, in Christ there is one destiny for all and one foundation for human dignity and freedom; in Christ there can be no distinction of slave and free, Jew and Gentile, Greek and barbarian, male and female. These distinctions do not cease to exist; they cease to be definitive of the dignity, destiny and potential of the community members. Moreover, Christians will not kill or harm or go to law to defend their claims.

In their own non-aggressive, non-violent way, these Christians of the first three centuries were introducing radical questions and radical reform of structures into the culture of pagan antiquity. It should cause little wonder that they were feared and persecuted by the empire, for they were bringing about a revolution all the more sure and drastic for the fact that it was not a rebellion and cost no lives other than their own at the hands of their persecutors. It should also cause little wonder that by the beginning of the fourth century the empire could only survive by ending hostilities and joining common cause with the Christians in their structuring of a society based on justice, peace and community. We know, as we look backward, that it turned out not to be quite as simple as that, but we also know that the Christians of the fourth century bent all their energies to the shaping of what seemed to them a Christian world, indeed what eventually gave rise to the term and notion of "Christendom."

It was as this symbiosis of Christendom developed that Christian energies and devotion were called forth to a new critical function. It is of no little interest to us today to observe the ways in which that critical function was carried out. There were, of course, those who exercised leadership within the system, trying to mold it to a more Christian pattern, and this was the case with most of the bishops as well as some great civic leaders. There were also those who challenged ill-used power directly, such as Ambrose of Milan with the Emperor Theodosius, or who challenged undue and ill-used wealth in their preaching, as Ambrose also did from his cathedral pulpit. But there were some who carried out their critique as Christians had always done, by joining themselves into a counter-cultural community living as best they could by the values and principles of the Gospel. Such were the communities of desert hermits and later of monastic groups. Such also were lay groupings like that of the women who associated with Paula of Rome.

One of the ways in which this expressed itself by the fifth century was in the effort to lessen the horrors and cruelties of war. At this time wars appeared inevitable as the empire struggled against the barbarians, but the wanton cruelties that went far beyond the needs of defense could not be accepted as part of the changeless rhythm of history by Christians. What we came to call by the quite inaccurate name of "just war theory" was offered by Augustine of Hippo precisely as a restraint both on the decision to go to war and on the ways that wars were conducted. Out of the experience of the life of the Christian community, particularly during the centuries of persecution, came that leap of creative imagination that grasped the possibility of human growth beyond the need for wars by extension of diplomacy and law. Augustine's rules of restraint did not proceed simply from his own philosophical or practical reflections, but from the maturity of Christian community experience upon which he could draw.

With the collapse and disintegration of the old empire in the West, Christian spirituality took a new turn, doing something rather unexpected. It embraced and preserved and integrated into itself much of the old pagan philosophy, law, literature and culture. There were some who had adopted certain of the pagan philosophies into Christian theology in earlier times, but there were no precedents for the kind of wholesale acceptance that we find, for instance, in Boethius. We might well ask why so much that was considered hostile to Christian life and spirit before was now adopted as its support and ally. Here, also, the Christian community is not so much repeating the attitudes and behavior of the past as forging a new way for a changing future. Now that the pagan culture was no longer the property of the ancient pagans, it could serve well as a vehicle to preserve the Christian heritage and the living process of Christian tradition against the new inroads of the contemporary pagans, the barbarians whose threat to Christianity was quite different. This has, of course, some analogy in our own time, for much that threatened our faith in the past and presented problems for Christian living has become quite harmless, as for instance with the Copernican theory of the universe, and the Darwinian theory of evolution. There is often a call to consider movements of thought and action and organization around us in a new light for a new age.

The example from the past can never be uncritically followed in subsequent ages because the context for action and decision is never the same. Throughout the medieval period, there was on the one hand the sense of Christendom which we have clearly lost in our experience of plurality, and there was on the other hand a persistent struggle between the ecclesiastical and the secular power which has taken on entirely new forms in our own times. Likewise, there was a certain tension between the continuous theological discourse of the Scholastics from which women were almost systematically excluded, and the lively and colorful devotional traditions and strands of spiritual theology in which women such as the German nuns, the Flemish and English mystics and the Italian Catherines played very active roles. These women are to us more admirable than imitable, precisely because we as contemporary women are not excluded from the mainstreams of theology and there is therefore no reason to build a spirituality without explicit theological foundations. Yet the inspiration of outstanding medieval women remains as fresh in our own times as it has been ever since their time.

Perhaps the most surprising aspect of the Reformation and immediate post-Reformation centuries is the fierce antagonisms felt and expressed between so many deeply spiritual people acting in complete good faith. It is for us to try to understand the positions from which they looked upon the issues and to try to sympathize with their goals and intentions. Certainly it is not for us to continue their hostilities and make them our own. For us, especially since the Second Vatican Council, all kinds of new possibilities have emerged for ecumenism and for reconciliations in many directions. Our best loyalty to the tradition in this case is in moving away from the patterns of mutual distrust and exclusion of the post-Tridentine era. But there is another aspect of that era that we do well to note. It is the universal concern among the reformers, whether Lutheran, Calvinist, Anabaptist or Catholic, to bring about a general return to personal prayer, deeper personal faith, a more genuinely Christian life-style, and a more serious study of doctrine. As much as they may have expressed hostility toward one another, there is a strong undercurrent of common purpose.

In retrospect we can recognize it, and it gives us a very different approach today from that which was possible for most Christians in the post-Tridentine era.

We have behind us now some centuries of doubt and anxiety in which modern philosophies and modern democratic regimes appeared to be in conflict with Christian life and faith. We have behind us a century or so of apparent conflict between science and technology on the one hand and the traditions of Christian teaching on the other. But we are past that now. As we look back we can see what appeared once to be contradictions but turned out to be complementarities. We can see what appeared to be threats but turned out to be promises, and led us in fact to deeper understanding of our faith and deeper appreciation and discernment of what is involved in Christian life.

## A "Usable Past" for Christian Women

From all of this there emerges the important question as to how we are to discern or identify the "usable past" that provides us with models, with insights, with warnings, with hope and challenge. Concerning the whole history, perhaps the most important insight that emerges is the extent to which Christian life is not a blueprint but a challenge to discernment. Each age and each generation faces its own problems and questions, and these have never been solved before just because they are new problems and new questions. But a second insight that emerges is that the truly, fruitfully Christian answers to these new challenges are based on continuity of the tradition—a continuity of hope, of experience, of fellowship, of prayer and of constant return to the sources in order to illuminate both the nature of the new questions and their relationship to the ancient faith. A third insight would seem to be the inextricably interwoven character of the personal and the societal dimensions of all the challenges that are presented to Christian spirituality: to relate well to God is to relate well among people on all levels of social complexity; to turn to God is in the last analysis to turn toward and not away from people; to acknowledge dependence upon God is to accept the full responsibility of interdependence with other people without exception and in all their needs.

When we ask whether there is a particular "usable past" for Christian women, we must acknowledge that the lives and deeds and impact of women have not been recorded and preserved for us in the same profusion as those of men. This is, of course, true of secular histories, but especially so of religious histories. There are many reasons for this. Most historical interest has centered upon public life whereas the customary division of labor until relatively modern times kept the activities of most women enclosed within the family circle. The examples that are recorded for us are therefore even more exceptional than in the case of men, for whom truly ordinary lives were not recorded either. Moreover, the focus of religious histories has commonly been upon affairs of the institutional churches precisely as institutions. The systematic exclusion of women from ordination and from positions of hierarchic authority therefore guarantees that in these histories we read little or nothing about women. This is less true, however, of histories of spirituality which have consistently taken note of monastic communities and of their outstanding members, and of lay Christians who initiated works of piety or charity or otherwise attracted attention among their contemporaries. In this there has been no reason for sexual discrimination, so that we really do have living examples in considerable detail, hampered only by the fact that the literary genres of hagiography of particular periods were not always understood and appreciated in subsequent ages.

Allowing for the inevitable bias in the available data, we can nevertheless draw some conclusions. Just because they were excluded from much of conventional public life, and from ordination and hierarchic authority, those Christian women who were recognized as memorable and whose lives and deeds were recorded have tended to emerge as more strongly counter-cultural in their attitudes, expectations, relationships and actions. Leadership of domination was frequently not open to them, nor were titles that inspire awe and create psychological distance. That left open the specifically Christian options of ministry, service, horizontal leadership by inspiration, invitation and community bonds of support. Similarly, conventional priestly and governing roles were usually closed to them, so it left open options for a more prophetic style than is usually possible to those who fill official positions and must play the conventional roles. And because existing offices in the Church were not assigned to them for most of history, women were often in a better position to notice what was being left undone and who was being left out in the pastoral practice of the institutional Church.

It is not surprising, therefore, that when we do have records of the work and impact of Christian women on their societies, that impact tends to be prophetic, radical in its implications for the social structures of the society in the long run, and, in terms of the social dynamics, a movement from below. Examples that come to mind immediately are the many initiatives for care of the indigent sick, which led eventually to the acceptance of the idea that each society, each nation, is responsible for universal health care for its citizens without reference to their ability to pay, with all the implications for tax and insurance structures and for government intervention which that accepted belief implies. Another example is that of the many small beginnings of schooling for the children of the poor, including the orphaned and the homeless, leading as it did eventually to almost universal literacy, public school systems, and a general belief that education is a basic right for all, with the far-reaching consequences which that has for possibilities of real democracy, of economic and geographic mobility, of trade unions and other ways of broad-based participation in the shaping of the economy and the social structures. Such initiatives for health care and education, commonly taken by women who saw them as expressions of faith called forth by the immediate circumstances in which they lived, also had long-term consequences which were like slow earthquakes in all of Western society, and which through colonization and international organizations have now become a challenge to the whole world.

Perhaps one of the most interesting aspects of the recorded deeds and impact of Christian women in the past is their concern for peace. From the unsuccessful efforts of Clotilde of the Franks, through a history that includes Elizabeth of Hungary, Elizabeth of Portugal, and Catherine of Siena, down to the peace protests of Dorothy Day and the women of Greenham Common, striving for peace and reconciliation of hostile parties has been characteristic of the lives of noted Christian women. Because of their general exclusion from power, the motivation of women's peace efforts has not come from the desire for unhampered, unqualified control of a country or situation after the manner of the famous Pax Romana of ancient times. Rather it has arisen from compassionate horror of the pain and suffering and bereavement that war causes, often to those who have least stake in the outcome.

## Women's Spirituality Today

The all-important question, of course, is what inspiration and implications we might draw for our own times. A most significant conclusion is certainly that as long as women are systematically excluded from ordination and from the institutionalized positions of leadership and decision-making in the Church, this has some advantages as well as the more obvious disadvantages. To be deprived of the power of domination, to have little or no access to bullying power, to be unable to compel or persuade by threat or use of institutional sanctions, is necessarily to be thrown back upon other resources. And that may well be to discover that divine power, the power of grace, is of a very different kind, effective inasmuch as it empowers and liberates human freedom—freedom for self-transcendence, freedom for true community with others, freedom for God and for God's purposes in creation and history. On the other hand, to have access to bullying power is inevitably to be sorely tempted to use it. But it is not Christ's way. Because of our Church organization, Christ's way by empowerment of human freedom to transcend is likely to be more immediately apparent to women.

Looked at positively, the characteristic possibilities for a spirituality of Christian women that can really make a Christian difference in a troubled world seem to be concerned particularly with prayer, compassion, solidarity and creative imagination. These are qualities and components which bridge the gap between the available models in the tradition of the past and the situation of contemporary women with their far greater access to positions of power and public persuasion. The opportunities are much enhanced for us in our own times, but the strictures under which our forebears worked seem in some ways to make the issues clearer. The question for us in our own times is how to make the best use both of the wider scope

26

offered to us and of the insight that we can derive from the past with the narrower scope that it offered to women.

The challenge which many of us have come to see as immediate and difficult is that of moving beyond submissive passivity in the affairs of society without at the same time indulging in angry rejection of the traditions of our faith or in aggressively competitive self-promotion which moves against rather than with the redemption of the world. It is clearly necessary to find ways of innovating, using initiative and exerting leadership, which are not based upon personal anger and hostility, and which do not seek to dominate or to seize exclusive privileges. In other words, it is necessary to avoid entering into competition for what have been seen as male prerogatives in a sinful history based upon bullying, and therefore it is necessary to discern new possibilities for quite different ways of social organization and community structures and cooperation. This calls for more than determination and aggressive energy; it also calls for contemplative sensitivity out of which new configurations can be imagined. It calls for a deeply rooted creativity.

Another problem or challenge which faces us in our own days is that of disentangling what is biologically determined as specifically feminine from that which is culturally prescribed, and distinguishing both of these from what makes up the Christian vocation of women. There are no easy answers to this. The biological component of sexual determination is, as we now come to realize, not static but responds to natural environment, nutritional factors, activity, culture and other spiritual factors. Indeed, the biological component can be extensively modified by deliberate human intervention. It has at some times in the past been generally accepted that women tend to be emotionally unstable, dependent, physically fragile and intellectually inferior to men. We have now discovered that good health care and social encouragement eliminate all these attributes. The basic factors that do not change in the bi ological determination are: the sexual complementarity of women and men, which allows for strong horizontal bonds in the human community, and the capacity for childbearing, which allows for strong vertical bonds across generations.

The culturally prescribed is usually based on these more basic biological factors, but is also tailored to the economy, ecology and political structure of each society. One of the most important foundations for a true personal spirituality is an unhurried, calm, non-violent, but fearlessly radical critique of the sex-role definitions of one's own society in the light of the Christian vocation.[5] The reason for the importance of such a critique is the fact that we live within a history of sin that distorts the truth of our existence in very persuasive ways. Every Christian life must be based on an analysis of one's society and situation which tries to discern what is God's good creation, what is the consequence of a history of sin, and what is already in the order of redemption because it has been touched and transformed by grace. Within a Christian context our criterion for all three is to be found in the person, life, teaching and death of Jesus Christ. Therefore it is found by an earnest quest for a deeper understanding of Jesus by meditation on Scripture, by study of available commentary and history, and by the contacts in the community of believers.

In the foregoing context, it is clear that the discernment of the Christian vocation of women in our own times is a dynamic, progressive, contextually varied and quite difficult task. It requires in the first place a certain clarity about the basic Christian teachings, namely revelation, creation, sin and redemption, Christology and grace, Church and sacramentality, and the hoped for outcomes of the redemptive history both for the world and for the individual. It is only in the context of these teachings and the large framework of interpretation of reality which they set that any vocational question can come into focus. But within that context that further determination must really be made on the basis of two questions: what are the needs of the community and what is the capacity of this individual or group to respond to those needs? Where the two intersect, the call of God is to be found. But this implies that a vo-

31

cation is not a call issued once in a lifetime, leaving the rest blueprinted and dispensing of the need for further discernment. Rather it suggests that vocational choices are being made and must be made continuously throughout one's life.

As in the case of individuals, so with the question of the vocation of Christian women taken as a class. It is not a determination to be made once, forever eliminating the need for further discernment. Rather it is a discernment to be made continuously throughout the generations of Christian history—a discernment to be made within each particular cultural and economic and socio-political situation. When we try to make such a communal discernment of vocation for Christian women within the North American situation in our own days, then we must certainly take into account the wealth that is at our disposal, the extent to which we have been liberated from back-breaking, soul-destroying, exhausting physical work, the civic rights and participation which we enjoy, the educational advantages which we have had, and the world of desperate needs which surrounds us in our times. There is no doubt that we are liberated from some of the truly exhausting work of housewives and mothers of the past and that we therefore have unprecedented opportunities to participate actively in the affairs of the larger society, through volunteer work, through professional or business careers and through political activity. There is also no doubt that the educational advantages we have enjoyed equip us for acquiring a good understanding of issues concerning peace and the continuing armaments build-up, and issues concerning the plight of the poor, the oppressed, refugees, political prisoners and populations undergoing famine.

It is, then, above all a time for individual and communal discernment on the part of Christian women of our times who have enjoyed a privileged education and are placed within the economically privileged, relatively leisured class in a democratically organized society that offers women great social freedom and, on the whole, great respect. Because it is a time of rapid changes in society and rapid communication across the whole world, the call for continuing discernment moves swiftly from crisis to crisis, opportunity to opportunity, and human need to human need. There are no blueprints, but there are those characteristic aspects of Christian life that bridge the gap between the models from our past and the demands beckoning from our future. Most particularly we might note: prayer, compassion, solidarity and imagination.

## A Life of Prayer

Christian life has at all times been marked as a life of prayer. But for long centuries of our history, prayer was seen primarily as a way of withdrawing from engagement in human affairs and the dilemmas and tragedies and responsibilities of human society. That is certainly not the kind of prayer called for in our times, even among contemplative religious communities. Clearly, our prayer should be such that it does not evade the ultimate Christian demand which is that of charity, of love of God which is expressed most unambiguously in loving care for the most needy, justice for the most oppressed, and peace in human society. This is a dynamic function of prayer: to give rise to a more completely, less exclusively or selectively loving activity in the world.

There are elements of our Church experience and of our less critical acceptance of what is going on around us that somehow suggest that to be prayerful in one's life is to be serenely accepting of whatever is happening, of whatever is the present order of things. What is forgotten in this attitude is that we live in a world that is much distorted by the consequences of evil deeds so that we cannot equate whatever is with the will of God. Prayer has a critical function. It is that encounter with God, that surrender to God's word, in which we are strengthened and steadied to see the world as it really is, distinguishing what is of God's good creating treasured and enhanced by human cooperation with the divine, from what is humanly fashioned in rejection of divine harmony and the divine focus. There is so much confusion in our human history and society, even in those structures that are supposed to guarantee justice and good order, that it is not easy to achieve enough psychological distance and enough spiritual balance to judge what is going on with the eyes of Jesus Christ. It is an arduous task to achieve independence from the grasp that the present order of things has over our understanding and expectations. But it is the function of prayer to enable us to see prophetically, to be prophetic and to act prophetically, evaluating what is by the light of what ought to be.

It has long been said that prayer has four aspects: adoration, thanksgiving, contrition and petition. That is certainly so, but it should not obscure the fact that the first purpose of an intimate conversation is to get to know the other and to reveal oneself to the other. The by-product of an intimate conversation is that one comes to know oneself better and to see one's relationship to the world differently. The by-product of a really good intimate conversation is empowerment and liberation. Such a conversation issues in easier, less self-conscious relationships with others in which one has more attention to spare for their words and their needs. It also results in greater self-possession, greater sense of purpose, in bolder clearer vision and in more energy to act. Such, of course, should be our prayer, and such it will be if we return constantly to the sources in Scripture and study them with a passion for intimate acquaintance with the person and the vision of Jesus Christ.

## CHRISTIANITY IS COMPASSION

To know the person and vision of Jesus is to be aware of another dimension. It is for that reason, surely, that his earliest followers, devout Jews, began to do the impossible, namely to attribute divinity to him. Throughout the ages we have tried and failed to name that quality that assures us of the divinity of Jesus. But we have acknowledged that it is not so much a matter of knowing what God is like and then finding that that is what Jesus is like. Rather it is a matter of having inadequate, fearful notions of what God is like, and then finding that Jesus overturns and invalidates all of these ideas. When the dust settles over our broken idols we find that life has acquired new meaning at a far deeper level, more intimately pervasive of our whole experience, and that the person of Jesus is at the center of the change and of the meaning.

When we try in the course of the centuries to disentangle the elements of this experience, we call Jesus divine and begin to recognize in a new way the attributes ascribed to God in the Hebrew Scriptures: power and compassion, creative energy and patience, sovereign transcendence and intimate, even passionate concern. All of these become alive and palpable in the person of Jesus as his first followers met him and knew him and as he appears in the Gospel portraits and the memory of the Church community to this day. But in our times, perhaps the most important and inclusive of these is the quality of compassion. Compassion means more than feeling sorrow over the suffering of another. It means entering deeply into the experience of the other. As we look back through centuries of Christian prayer and Christian experience, and also of Christian failings, it becomes clearer that what we have seen in the person of Jesus is the divine entering deeply into our experience, to understand it and possess it from within, transforming its possibilities and strengthening its hope, giving it a new center and new impulse.

We may even say that as we come to terms with the person and the message of Jesus in our own lives, compassion comes to be more clearly at the center of what Christianity is supposed to be (and commonly fails to be). Sin and sinfulness in the world are always a matter of uncentering God's purpose and replacing it with one's own projects. This builds a culture and a society that cannot work, cannot be at peace, cannot fill people's most important needs, because it is many-centered, which means uncentered. Many incompatible projects are in competition in our world. To pursue them, people must and do exclude awareness of the needs and experiences of others. People must and do build walls of isolation which exclude certain others who thereupon "do not count." Women are particularly well placed to understand this and to appreciate the consequences for individuals and for the fabric of society, because there have been so many contexts in which all of us, half the human race, have been excluded and defined as irrelevant, as not "counting."

The suffering of such systemic exclusion of those who have gone before us with whom we can readily identify, by those in other contemporary cultures with whom we must try to identify, and by those among us whose gifts and calling are not acknowledged or honored, is an experiential basis for working toward a clearer understanding of what it is that is awry in our world. It is an experiential basis for an understanding of compassion as the redemptive answer to all that is awry. To enter deeply into the experience of the other, of any other, without exclusion or discrimination is indeed to unravel the apparently unredeemable hatreds, oppressions and miseries of our world. When we look back over what is known of the lives of the outstanding Christian women mentioned at the outset of this presentation, it is clear that a central and powerful driving force that motivated them all was this kind of compassion.

## Solidarity Is the Future

It is not accidental that one of the greatest contemporary struggles with tyranny and injustice has been fought under the name of "Solidarity." Redemptive compassion issues in solidarity, and the structures by which redemption is brought about, are structures of solidarity. If sin is the centering of private projects to the disregard of what these do to other people, and with consequences of feuds and wars, oppression and needless sufferings, fear and insecurity, violence and chaos, then redemption is the process of undoing all this by the reconstruction of a society, a world, a network of relationships that respect the solidarity of the human race as created and destined by God. We are far from this reconstruction and it may seem that the project is quite hopeless, yet quiet observation assures us that every small effort or initiative in this direction is almost immediately immensely fruitful.

In our own society, and often under secular auspices, there have been and continue to be all manner of movements for "sisterhood," that is, the experience of solidarity, community, and mutual support among women. It is true that sometimes these have been built upon sheer anger and resentment, upon rejection of religious and civic authority and institutions. Clearly, anything built upon hatred is not very strong in the long run, though it may have the power of desperation in the short run. Moreover, anything built upon wholesale rejections is not well situated to work toward ever-widening, non-exclusive circles of community solidarity. However, most of these initiatives are really not of that kind, but are built upon some spontaneous movements toward mutual support and encouragement and solidarity. Even where such initiatives do not originate from Christian spirituality, we need to recognize them for what they are—in their own ways redemptive, in their own ways allies to the Christian task.

In many parts of the world a more radical movement toward solidarity is underway in the forms of basic communities, some of which are basic Christian communities. They are formed, more often than not, among the poor, sometimes among the very poor. Beginning sometimes from the need for protection, sometimes from the desire to pray together, and other times from an urgency to better wretched conditions, these groups have much to teach the whole Church and especially those of us who are more economically privileged. Often they have rediscovered the Gospel in great depth. They have rediscovered the absolute inseparability of the love of God from the love of neighbor, along with the realization that this notion of "neighbor" cannot exclude anyone, not even the present oppressor, and therefore calls for the acknowledgement of ultimate solidarity of the whole human race, of the whole creation. In some cases such outreach across barriers of wealth and class struggle has been and must be the particular task of women because they have a greater freedom to move across class barriers and establish bonds. There is much to be learned from the experience of the basic Christian communities in third world countries concerning the practical shape of the redemption in our times.

The more the sufferings and fears and problems of the world flash rapidly across our television screens and appear in our morning papers, the more urgently Christian spirituality appears as essentially a matter of compassion expressing itself in widening patterns of solidarity. Any other approach rapidly becomes so depressing and discouraging that it has a paralysing effect, sending people into their private seclusion in flight from problems that appear too big even to be acknowledged. But the Christian response is that of solidarity, built in any direction in which there are possibilities for it, and in many directions in which there do not appear to be possibilities for it.

## CREATIVE IMAGINATION

From the beginning, Christians have known that they were called upon to do the impossible. But when we look at Scripture and at the history of the Christian community, we can see a pattern in the way former impossibilities became subsquent realizations. The dynamics of the prophetic are in the creative imagination. The Scriptures themselves provide rich imagery and symbolism. They are replete with stories of classic universality, and with personalities that lend themselves as prototypes even across cultures and centuries. Catholic tradition has particularly appreciated and treasured this in its promotion of the sacramental principle. That is to say, Catholic tradition has taken note of the extent to which the human imagination needs to be educated in a world distorted by the consequences of sin and sinfulness.

When we look at the world about us, we never simply record what is there. We interpret. The society in which we live teaches us certain lines of interpretation according to which we consider things good or bad, normal or abnormal, more or less desirable, even more or less reasonable. The traditions, values and expectations of our own society tend to hold us captive. In a pluralist society we may think we have escaped this because many alternatives present themselves. Yet even pluralistic society limits the range of those alternatives in ways that those within that society do not easily recognize. In a world and a history distorted by sin, the range of alternatives which a society allows is always to some extent athwart the divine purpose, but it is very difficult to imagine anything beyond or outside the permitted range. A fundamental task of Christian spirituality is imagination. It is the task of breaking the process of interpretation wide open to glimpse entirely new and different possibilities of human life and relationships.

Imagination is exercised in influential ways through literature, through the visual and performing arts, through music, but also through human relationships, social structures, technology and science. Christian spirituality is related to all of these in two ways: it should inform them and it should be informed by them. It should inform them not in the sense that works of art and science should be deliberately used to moralize, catechize or set out to defend the faith, but rather that Christians steeped in the Scriptures and deeply influenced by prayer and by the imperatives of charity should pursue the arts as a vocation, should engage in political process and policy, and should devote themselves to technological invention and scientific research. They need only be fully what they are and take the field seriously for what it is, and theredemption of the society through the expanding imagination will happen because the channels for redemptive grace run through us if we allow them to be open. But it is also true that the various expressions of human ingenuity in these various fields need to inform Christian spirituality and to ensure that it is dealing with the real world and the real problems of real people—to ensure that Christian spirituality is authentic and not an escape into a dream world.

Throughout history women have been allowed rather freely into the realms of imagination in the arts and literature and sometimes even in science, but in previous generations they were seldom taken seriously. Their interests and activities were allowed as hobbies and accomplishments and this alone justified the time and energy and resources spent upon them. In our own days, women are generally taken seriously as contributors to the professions and the arts and public life. From the point of view of Christian women and the difference they can make to a troubled and disoriented world, this new respect and freedom in the public sphere is a great opportunity which also carries its subtle temptations. Obviously, it offers opportunities for more effective action and wider influence. But it also carries the temptation to look on the new openings simply as career opportunities and occasions for self-advancement, rather than looking upon them as matters of Christian vocation. And it carries the temptation to enter the public sphere in a purely competitive spirit seeking enhancement of prestige, wealth and power, rather than entering the public sphere in a spirit of service, of compassion, of solidarity. To yield to these temptations is a great loss. It closes the imagination, locking people into the established pattern, rather than opening up new possibilities.

It would seem that because of our history and because of the turning point at which we of this generation stand, Christian women have a calling to preserve their freedom of spirit in using the creative imagination, in the way that they have possessed it in their socially and politically powerless past, but at the same time to express that freedom and creativity with power in the public sphere. It is this combination of spiritual freedom and social opportunity and power which holds promise of a new and creative way of building bridges of reconciliation toward world peace, of restructuring the systems of society which impoverish and marginate the powerless, and of sowing "seeds of unity and hope and salvation for the whole human race."[6]

There is so much that Christian women by prayer, compassion, solidarity and creative imagination can do for a troubled world.

## Notes

1. As evidenced, for instance, in *The Republic*.
2. See entries under these names in *The International Dictionary of Women's Biography,* ed. Jennifer Uglow and Frances Hinton (New York: Continuum, 1982).
3. For scholarly and interesting examination of what we really know of the women in the earliest churches, i.e., those of the New Testament, see Elisabeth Schüssler Fiorenza, *In Memory of Her* (N.Y.: Crossroad, 1983). For testimony concerning the following centuries (the patristic period), see Roger Gryson, *The Ministry of Women in the Early Church* (Collegeville: Liturgical Press, 1980). For the medieval period, see Peter Dronke, *Women Writers of the Middle Ages* (Cambridge: University Press, 1984).

4. Basic biographical facts for most of these women, as well as further bibliography concerning them, are available in Uglow and Hinton, *op. cit.*
5. For biblical and theological foundations for such reflection, see George Tavard, *Women in Christian Tradition* (Notre Dame: University of Notre Dame Press, 1973).
6. This is the formulation of the essential task of the Church given in Vatican Council II's *Lumen Gentium* (*Dogmatic Constitution on the Church*), Part II, n. 9.

MONIKA K. HELLWIG, LLB, M.A., Ph.D, is professor of theology at Georgetown University. After a childhood spent as a refugee from eastern Europe, and university studies in England, she was engaged in social service for some time before becoming a theologian. She is the single parent of three adopted children, and the author of a number of books including *Understanding Catholicism* (Paulist Press), *The Eucharist and the Hunger of the World* (Paulist Press), and *Jesus the Compassion of God* (Michael Glazier, Inc.).